*2000 Years of British Coins and Medals*

# 2000 Years of British Coins and Medals

### John Kent

Published for the Trustees of the
British Museum

by British Museum Publications Limited

© 1978, The Trustees of the British Museum

ISBN 0 7141 0842 1 (*cased*)

ISBN 0 7141 0845 6 (*paper*)

Published by British Museum Publications Ltd.
6 Bedford Square, London WC1B 3RA.
Designed by James Shurmer

Printed in Great Britain by Billing & Sons Ltd
Worcester and London

Set in Bembo by Computer Photoset Ltd, Birmingham

NOTE
*Illustrations in Chapters 1–15 are all
twice actual size; in Chapters 16–28
they are at actual size.*

British Library Cataloguing in Processing Data
Kent, John
    2000 years of coins and medals.
    1. British Museum 2. Coins,
    British–Exhibitions
    3. Medals, British–Exhibitions
    I. Title II. British Museum III. Two thousand
    years of coins and medals
    737.4'9'41        CJ2474.2.L/
    737'.2            CJ6102.2.L/

4

# Preface

It is now fifty-five years since the publication of the third edition of the general *Guide* to the exhibitions of the Department of Coins and Medals, and almost eighty years from the appearance of H. A. Grueber's monumental *Handbook of the Coins of Great Britain and Ireland*. Though much of its classification has been superseded, the latter remains a standard descriptive work on the British coinage, and as such has been thought worth reprinting within the last few years.

The modern concept of an exhibition differs widely from that of our predecessors. Coins and medals are now seen as part of a historical process with inter-related political, artistic, social and economic aspects. These relationships are explored in the text and in the accompanying illustrations, which aim to give the visitor to the gallery visual points of reference between the coinage and the other arts. The widest possible limits of time have been chosen, in order to stress historical continuity. A much wider and better informed public than was formerly the case now desires instructive and thought-provoking material. The Department has tried to meet this challenge, drawing on the experience of its officers, gained in answering public enquiries and in lecturing to numismatic societies.

In the majority of instances, actual coins and medals are exhibited. However, in cases where it has been necessary to display the obverse and reverse of the same piece, electrotype facsimiles have been used. The originals, which are regularly required by students for research, may be examined in the departmental Students' Room.

John Kent
*Deputy Keeper, Department of Coins and Medals*

1

2

7

25

33

35

# 1. Celtic Britain, c.70BC–AD43

The earliest currency in Britain appeared in the first half of the first century BC. Julius Caesar, who invaded Britain in 55 and 54 BC, tells us that the Britons of his day had coinage of gold and iron. Iron bars, believed to have been used as currency have been found on a number of sites in Britain.

The earliest gold coins, circulating in south and east England, belong to a succession of types struck by the Belgic tribes of north-west France (2–6). Their design is derived from that of the gold stater of Philip II of Macedon, 351–336 BC (1), whose basic type of Apollo and charioteer was revived and much copied in the second century BC. Also early in date and Gallic in their inspiration are the so-called 'speculum' coins (35) of the Thames Valley and East Anglia. In and after Caesar's time British tribes or dynasties in the south-east struck copies of Continental coins of steadily declining weight and fineness, and for a while of increasing barbarity of style (7–13).

This decline was largely arrested by the rise, after 50 BC, of two paramount kingdoms, the Atrebates of Sussex and Hampshire and the Catuvellauni of Hertfordshire and Essex. Anonymous issues of these peoples (14,15) were followed, not later than c. 20 BC, by coins inscribed with the names of successive kings. Coin-finds plotted on distribution maps show how the territory of the Atrebatic kings Commios (16), Tincommios (17) and Verica (18,19) dwindled in the face of the attacks of the Catuvellaunian kings Tasciovanus (20–24) and Cunobelinus (25–29) shortly before the Roman invasion of AD 43; Roman sources described Cunobelinus as 'King of the Britons'. By this time, the growth of internal commerce had led to the development of coinages of silver and bronze.

Of the less important tribes, the Durotriges of Dorset and Wiltshire had been one of the first to adopt a coinage. By 50 BC this contained little if any gold (11), and eventually degenerated into barbarous cast bronzes (12,13). The Dobunni of Gloucestershire (30,31) and the Iceni of Norfolk and Suffolk (32,33) struck a little base gold and a fair amount of silver, some of it inscribed with the names of chiefs. The Coritani of Leicestershire and Lincolnshire (34) retained the use of base gold and struck only a little silver; some of their coins, too, bear the names of chiefs.

# 2. Roman Britain

Few Roman coins entered Britain before the invasion of AD 43. The needs of the occupying army and the officials, however, soon required the large-scale import of Roman currency, though for a while its relative shortage was supplemented by extensive forgery. Roman coins rapidly superseded native issues in the areas directly ruled; in the short-lived client kingdoms, such as that of the Iceni, both currencies co-existed for a while.

During the first century AD the normal coin find on Romano-British sites is the *as* (6,7) and its imitations. *Sestertii* (4,8) and *dupondii* (5,9) are characteristic of the second century, though rarely of a later date than Commodus (AD 180–192); bronze coins continued to circulate down to the reign of Postumus (AD 260–269) (18). Silver *denarii* remained current for long periods, those of Mark Antony (1) for over 250 years.

The third century AD was marked by severe inflation, accompanied by depreciation of the coinage (12–15). In consequence, the very base silver of the years AD 260–275 and its numerous imitations (16–25) was both produced and lost in large quantities. Efforts to reform the currency and stabilize the economy enjoyed only passing success; the main coinage between *c.* AD 295 and 365 consisted of abundant and unstable issues of base silver which underwent frequent alterations of standard and of valuation, and at least three total demonetizations (16–34).

During the last half-century of Roman rule, a good silver coinage was once more available (Chap. 4); it was supported by spasmodic, but seemingly adequate, issues of small bronze pieces (32–37). The withdrawal of Roman government in the early fifth century AD meant that coins virtually ceased to enter Britain. Surviving silver coins were severely clipped, but all currency seems to have come to an end before the middle of the century.

The reverses of Roman coins were regularly used to draw public attention to the achievements or aspirations of the emperors. Britain was only infrequently mentioned, but allusions to imperial activity here can appropriately be found on coins of Claudius (AD 41–54) (2), Hadrian (AD 117–138) (10), Antoninus Pius (AD 138–161) (11), Commodus (AD 180–192) and Septimius Severus (AD 193–211) (12).

26    27

3

11

12

36

14

10

# 3. Rebels in Britain, AD286-296

The activities of Saxon pirates in British waters led to the establishment, in the late third century AD, of a powerful military command, based on a combination of troops, a fleet and a chain of forts. In AD 286 the commander of this force, Carausius, rebelled against Diocletian, the reigning emperor, and established himself in Britain. Here he set up two principal mints, London (1–10) and C . . . (14–23) (a town not identified with certainty). On the Continent too, where at first he held extensive territory, coins were struck for him at Rouen (29–31) and perhaps at Boulogne (24–28).

His early coins are of a very rough style (24–28), but later issues show great improvement. At first Carausius seems to have had little gold; his base silver coins were accompanied by silver pieces of much finer metal (12). In the second half of his reign these were discontinued in favour of a normal gold coinage (13,29).

In all things Carausius strove to make his government and coinage like that of the rest of the Empire. He assumed the consulship and had himself depicted in its robes of office (11,26); he brought his coins into line, in style and standard, with those of the Continent.

Carausius was faced by a constant threat from his Continental rivals, Diocletian and Maximian. In a vain effort to win their recognition he caused coins to be struck in their names (6,9,19,20) and on one celebrated issue, declared them to be his 'brothers' (14). The 'peace' constantly proclaimed on his coinage was denied to Carausius, and the loss of his Continental foothold in AD 293 was speedily followed by his assassination and replacement by his finance minister Allectus.

Allectus reigned for only three years, over an empire confined to Britain itself. His coinage from London (32–37) and C . . . (38–43) shows the mature style of his predecessor but towards the end of his reign suffers a marked reduction in size. It is not known whether this late coinage, which refers exclusively to Allectus' fleet (35,41–43,55), is the result of the usurper's shaky finances or is an attempt to bring his coinage into line with contemporary reforms in the rest of the Emire.

Britain was regained for the Central Empire in AD 296.

43

# 4. The London Mint in Roman Times

When Constantius I defeated and killed Allectus in AD 296, he closed the mint of C . . . , but retained that of London as part of a system whereby each group of provinces was served by its own mint. Early issues of the mint bear the explicit inscription LON (1,2), but between AD 297 and 307 London coins are not mint-marked and can be recognized only by their style (3–8).

London was an important mint under Constantine the Great (AD 306–337). His earliest coins often express his devotion to Mars, the god of war (15,16,19); from about AD 311 his principal attention was transferred to the Sun-god (21,23,30,34,37). Coins of this period sometimes bear the head of a colleague, usually his father-in-law Maximian (12,14,15) or his late father, Constantius I (d. AD 306) (18), honoured as a god.

In AD 312 Constantine defeated his rival Maxentius and annexed Italy and Africa north of the Sahara to his empire. The mint of London honoured this success by a series of coins celebrating his state entry into Rome (*Adventus*) (22,32,35), the unanimous loyalty of his troops (*Concordia*) (26), and the security (*Securitas*) brought by his rule (28).

Constantine now had but one surviving colleague, Licinius (42), Emperor of the East. In AD 317 two sons of Constantine, Crispus and Constantine II (46,47), and the son and namesake of Licinius were raised to the rank of Caesar, and duly appeared on the coinage. Shortly after this event, the pagan deities cease to figure on the coins. In their place we find the abstract concepts of Victory, Valour, Peace and Foresight (49–62). In AD 324 the fall of Licinius left Constantine master of the whole Roman world. A final burst of coinage from London included issues for the Emperor's mother Helena (63), his wife Fausta (64), and his three sons (62). Then the mint closed, leaving Britain's currency needs to be met principally by the mints at Trier, Lyons and Arles.

The revolt of Magnus Maximus against Gratian in AD 383 led to a last brief opening of the mint in London, now officially named Augusta. Two extremely rare issues of gold (65) and silver (66) remind us that the insurrection broke out in Britain.

22

63

64

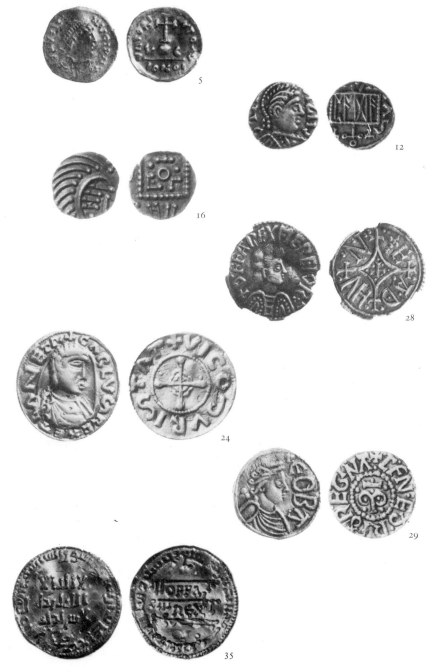

# 5. The First Coins of the English

After the abandonment of Britain by the Roman empire in the early fifth century AD, Roman coins ceased to circulate. Those which were dug up by farmers or entered the country as trade or loot served as ornaments rather than currency.

The growing stability of the major Anglo-Saxon kingdoms in the later sixth century AD led to the development of political relations with the Merovingian Franks of Gaul. This was reflected in the circulation in Anglo-Saxon England of small numbers of Frankish gold coins called tremisses. The St Martin's (Canterbury) hoard, of about AD 570 (1–4), has been plausibly associated with Bishop Liudhard, chaplain to Bertha, the Frankish queen of Aethelberht of Kent (AD 561–616).

By the start of the seventh century AD, Frankish gold coins were an established currency in south-east England; the Sutton Hoo ship-burial contained thirty-seven pieces dating from between about AD 580 and AD 620 (5–7). The first Anglo-Saxon English coinage, struck at London, Canterbury, and perhaps elsewhere, followed no later than about AD 630 (8–10). These coins were derived from Roman rather than Frankish pieces, and many bore no intelligible inscription.

The supply of Byzantine gold to the Franks dried up around AD 630, and their gold currency, as well as the derivative English series, rapidly became debased (12). Towards the end of the seventh century AD, its place was taken by small silver coins, called *denarii,* i.e. pennies (19,20). By the middle of the eighth century AD these were being minted at several centres, mainly in eastern and southern England; their designs were sometimes mere barbarous copies of earlier types, and sometimes fresh creations of considerable artistry (12–18).

In AD 751 Pepin, first king of the Frankish Carolingian dynasty, introduced his 'new penny' (21–23), larger, heavier and worth more than its predecessors. This standard was adopted by the moneyers of central and southern England in the years following AD 760 (25–32). Like its Frankish precursor, this coin bears the names of kings, the greatest of whom was Offa of Mercia (AD 757–796). These new silver pennies, bearing the name of the king whose authority they acknowledge and the moneyer by whom they were minted, set the pattern of English coinage for the next five hundred years. Occasional issues of gold were made (35), but did not enter into general circulation, while coinage of the old type continued unchanged in Northumbria (Chap. 7). On the Continent also rare gold coins were struck, for example by Charlemagne at Dorstadt (24).

1

6

9

12

16

17

# 6. Mercia and Kent, c.AD800-900

The supremacy over England enjoyed by Mercia at the death of Offa in AD 796 steadily declined under his successors. In AD 802 Wessex slipped from the grasp of Coenwulf (AD 796–821) (1), best known for his wars against the Britons of North Wales, and when Coenwulf's brother and successor Coelwulf I (AD 821–823) (2,3) was deposed, the ancient royal house of Mercia came to an end. Within a year Mercian overlordship in Kent and East Anglia had been swept away, during the disastrous reign of Beornwulf (AD 823–825) (4,5), a king not of the royal line. His successors, Ludica (AD 825–827) (6) and Wiglaf (AD 827–840) (7), preserved the integrity of their kingdom against Wessex; and thereafter good relations between the kingdoms were maintained until the fall of Mercia to the Danes c.875. Of the last three Mercian kings, Berhtwulf (AD 840–852) (8), Burgred (AD 852–874) (9), Ceolwulf II (AD 874–c.875) (10), little is known.

Most of the earlier Mercian coinage was struck at Canterbury. After AD 824 London was probably the principal Mercian mint, though under Burgred (all of whose known coins fall in the second half of his reign) Canterbury seems once more to have been available.

Until AD 824 the kings of Kent and the archbishops of Canterbury were virtual subjects of Mercia. The coins of Eadberht II (AD 796–798) (11) represent a revolt against Mercian rule, but Cuthred, Coenwulf's brother, (AD 798–807) (12,13) and Baldred (?AD 825) (14,15) were Mercian vassals. After the conquest by Wessex, Kent was ruled by under-kings of the Wessex royal house.

The archbishops of Canterbury during the period of Mercian supremacy, Jaenberht (AD 766–790) (Chap. 5) and Aethelheard (AD 793–805) (16) struck coins bearing the name of their overlord. The later archbishops Wulfred (AD 805–832) (17), Ceolnoth (AD 833–870) (18), Aethered (AD 870–889) (19) and Plegmund (AD 890–914) (20) were less obviously subordinate; their coinages are of autonomous princes, corresponding closely to those of the kings in form, if not in quantity.

20

# 7. East Anglia, Northumbria and the Vikings, c.AD700-950

The earlier kings of the East Angles who are known to us from their coins ruled under Mercian domination; such were Beonna (*c*. AD 760) (1), Ethelberht (d. AD 794) (2) and Eadwald (*c*. AD 796) (3). Freedom from Mercia was achieved by the defeat of Beornwulf in AD 825, and thereafter East Anglia was ruled by a series of independent kings, Aethelstan (*c*. AD 825) (4), Aethelward (*c*. AD 850) (5) and (St) Edmund (AD 855–870) (7). Edmund was killed by the Danes, many of whom settled in and ruled over his kingdom. The best-known was Guthrum, who after his submission to Alfred in AD 878 reigned under the baptismal name of Aethelstan (AD 880–890) (8,9). The evangelization of the Danes of East Anglia led to the issue of an extensive coinage in the name of the martyred St Edmund (*c*. AD 880–910) (10–12). East Anglia became part of the growing kingdom of the English during the reign of Edward the Elder (AD 899–924).

The earliest Northumbrian king of whom coins are known is Aldfrith (AD 685–704) (14); they are in the contemporary 'sceatta' tradition, with a strange animal type. Northumbria remained untouched by Offa's new penny. From about the middle of the eighth century AD to the fall of the kingdom to the Vikings in AD 867, a series of increasingly base pieces was struck in the names of Eadberht (AD 737–758) (15,16), Alhred (AD 765–774) (17,18), Eardwulf (AD 796–808) (19), Eanred (AD 808–841) (20,21), Aethelred II (AD 841–849) (22), Redwulf (AD 844) (23,24), Osberht (AD 849–867) (25) and others. The archbishops of York too had the privilege of coinage; we know of pieces struck by Ecgberht (AD 734–766) (26), Eanbald (AD 796–808), Wigmund (AD 837–854) (27) and Wulfhere (AD 854–900) (28). Almost all are of very base silver, but an exceptional gold *solidus*, based on Carolingian models, was struck for Wigmund.

After the Viking conquest of Northumbria, York became between *c*. AD 880–*c*.950 the seat of a succession of vigorous though precarious Danish and Norse rulers, of whom little is known. Cnut (29–32) and Siefred (33–36) were Danish rulers of the end of the ninth century AD. Sihtric (37), Anlaf (38) and Eric (39,40) disputed possession of York with the kings of England during the second quarter of the tenth century. A few anonymous coinages were produced in the northern Danelaw, amongst them ecclesiastical issues in the name of St Peter (41,42).

2

23

6

9

20

# 8. Wessex, AD825-959

The rise of the kingdom of Wessex to supremacy in England followed the collapse of Mercian power in AD 825. Ecgbeorht (AD 802–839), the long-established king of Wessex, occupied Kent and, for a short while, Mercia itself. His control of Canterbury, Rochester and, briefly, London ensured a steady issue of coinage (1,2). The coinage of his son Aethelwulf (AD 839–858) was also predominantly Kentish (3), and a great variety of types marks this reign. Of his four sons, Aethelbald (AD 858–860) had no coins. Those of Aethelberht (AD 858–866) (4) and Aethelred I (AD 866–871) (5) follow the same tradition. The latter's type is used by Burgred of Mercia (Chap. 6, no.9), and is also the earliest type of Alfred (AD 871–899).

Alfred's troubled reign ensured that the West Saxon dynasty would eventually become rulers of all England. It also led to much variety in and experimentation with the coinage. Alfred's special relationship with Rome, established when he visited the Pope with his father in AD 855, is reflected in his remarkable 'Alms' piece (6); its legend, ELIMO(SINA), may be compared with that on a denier of the Frankish king Pepin (Chap. 5, no.22). This 'Alms' piece is the approximate equivalent of seven ordinary pence.

Under Alfred, the mint name is found on a number of rare issues – Gloucester, Exeter (7), Winchester (10) and London (8,9). The latter are distinguished by a relatively elegant style and a carefully constructed monogram of the city name. Another fine piece, with the bust conceived on late Roman lines (11), comes from the first half of the reign, and shares its type with Ceolwulf II of Mercia. Towards the end of the reign, the coinage was greatly simplified (12,13). This basic pattern remained dominant for the next eighty years.

The subjection of all England to the rule of the house of Wessex went ahead under Edward the Elder (AD 899–924). His general coinage closely resembles the latest issues of his father (21,22), but a rare series of interesting and highly ornamented pieces was also coined in north-west England (15–20,23). A more general variant, used particularly in East Anglia, bore the king's effigy (14).

Coins of the later kings, Aethelstan (AD 924–939) (24–27), Eadmund (AD 939–946) (29–31), Eadred (AD 946–955) (32) and Eadwig (AD 955–959) (33–35), continue this pattern. Of special interest are the title 'King of All Britain' assumed by Aethelstan (26,27), and the unique penny (28) struck at Chester with the name of Howel Dda, the tributary king of North Wales.

1

14

18

21

22

31

22

38

# 9. Kings of All England, 959–1066

The reign of Edgar (AD 959–975) marks a turning-point in the English coinage. Throughout most of his reign, his pence conformed to the typology which had been evolved early in the tenth century (2,3), with essentially regional type variations. Almost at the end of his reign, however, he achieved the long-expressed ideal of the English kings, that there should be only one money throughout their realm. The new, uniform type was very simple: on the obverse, the royal bust and name; on the reverse, a small cross and names of moneyer and mint (1). The systematic declaration of mint as well as moneyer persisted into the reign of Edward I (see Chap. 12). The coinage is almost entirely of silver pence, though one or two gold pieces are known (5). Coinage of the small cross type continued through the reign of Edward the Martyr (AD 975–979) (4) into that of Ethelred II (The Unready) (979–1016). During Ethelred's reign began the system of periodic changes of type, at first about every six years, and later, under Edward the Confessor (1042–66) (22–36), about every three years. This practice, which lasted down to the reign of Henry II (see Chap. 11), seems to have been intended to ensure the maximum revenue to the king from the profits of coinage. Under Ethelred, the small cross type was twice repeated, suggesting the complete recall of earlier coins. Under later kings, however, successive types were radically distinguished from one another on both sides, and designs were seldom revived. Nonetheless, coins at this period tended to have relatively short lives in currency, rarely exceeding twenty years.

Reverse designs are usually based upon the cross. Obverses, with one exception, show the royal effigy. This may be partly derived from a Roman prototype (5,11,14,21–29,38), and may include such contemporary features as crown and sceptre, or helmet (19,20). In the second half of Edward the Confessor's reign, a more naturalistic effigy is adopted (30–37); an interesting variant is the enthroned king with orb and sceptre (32,33).

To execute this coinage policy, upwards of seventy mints were established. The conquest of England by the Danish dynasty of Cnut (1016–35) (17–19), Harold I (1035–40) (20), and Harthacnut (1040–42) (21) made no difference to the coinage, nor did the Norman victory over Harold II (1066) (38).

# 10. The Normans, 1066-1154

The Norman conquest made little initial impact on the English coinage, other than a substitution of the name of William for that of Harold. Only gradually did moneyers with Norman names begin to appear (27,40,42), and spellings influenced by the pronunciation of French-speaking clerks to occur beside Old English forms (38).

Thirteen types of penny bearing the name William are known. They are divided between William I (1066–87) (1–15) and William II (1087–1100) (16–23) on a proportional basis, as their order is established with reasonable certainty. The reign of William II is marked by a steady decline in the appearance of the coinage; both art and technique had sunk to a very low ebb by the accession of Henry I (1100–35) (24–34).

Brutal sanctions against moneyers who debased the coin had always existed. Under Henry, public confidence in the royal money reached the lowest level since the time of Edgar (see Chap. 9). The practice of snicking the edge of coins to test their fineness (27–29) became universal by the middle years of Henry I's reign, and at Christmas 1124 he carried out a purge of unparalleled severity. Most of the moneyers of England were condemned to mutilation, and the coinage of Henry's last three types (30–34) shows a significant improvement.

The troubled reign of King Stephen (1135–54) (35–46) was marked by less confusion in the coinage than might have been expected. Some coins of his first type garble the royal name, others show the use of erased dies. A rare series bears the name of the Empress Matilda, his challenger for the throne (45). Peculiar to this reign are special types associated with York (43,44), a few of which bear the name of a local magnate, Eustace FitzJohn (46).

45

46

# 11. The Early Plantagenets, 1154-1272

Henry II (1154–89) re-established and reinforced the strong personal rule of king. His decisive influence on the development of medieval government is reflected in changes in the coinage. The first issues to bear his name, the so-called Tealby type, began to be struck in 1158. Though not materially different in design or technique from their predecessors, they were struck without significant change for twenty-two years (1–4).

The process of type-immobilization was developed still further in the 'short-cross' pence, which began to be struck in 1180. They were scarcely beautiful, though new standards of evenness and legibility were demanded (5–7). Most important, stability was emphasized by the retention of Henry's name on issues of his sons, Richard I (1189–99) (8–10,13) and John (1199–1216) (12,14–16). Henry III (1216–72) continued this issue until 1247 (17,18). Approximate dates for the different phases of this coinage are established by documentary evidence, confirmed by stylistic criteria, such as the close relationship between the class V 'Henry' coins and the Irish pence which bear John's name (21). Other coins of this period remind us of the extensive possessions of the English kings in France (19,20).

In 1248 Henry III's shaky finances were boosted by a change in the coinage, on which the short-cross was replaced by one extending to the edge of the coin (23–34), ostensibly to deter clipping. The new type rapidly replaced the old, but after the few years of recoinage, only the mints of London and Canterbury remained really active; the numerous mints of Saxon and Norman England were by now anachronisms.

Of special interest is the abortive attempt in 1257 to introduce a gold coinage (22). It was current at first for twenty, and later for twenty-four pence, but no more than one issue was made, and few survive. Like John, Henry III also had an Irish coinage (35). The 'long-cross' coinage was also an immobilized type. Although it bore the name of Henry III–the first English coinage to bear the monarch's numeral–it continued to be struck down to 1279 (33,34).

22

3

23

12

19

35

24

42

# 12. Edward I, 1272–1307 and Edward II, 1307–27

For the first seven years of his reign, Edward I (1272–1307) continued the immobilized type of his father's coinage (see Chap. 11, nos.33–34). The reform which he undertook in 1279 fixed the form of English money down to the reign of Henry VII (1485–1509) (see Chap. 16). His coinage falls into two divisions. The first, struck largely between 1279 and 1285, included for the first time a full range of silver denominations – groat (fourpence) (19,20), penny (1–18), halfpenny (21–23) and farthing (24–26). The groat seems to have evoked no public demand, and was speedily discontinued. Halfpence and farthings were popular, for they did away with the need to cut pence into halves and quarters, a practice well attested from late Saxon times. They were, however, relatively unprofitable to produce, and down to the introduction of copper halfpence and farthings in the seventeenth century (Chap. 18, 19, 21), governments and moneyers were under repeated pressure to strike greater numbers of these desirable, unprofitable and easily lost pieces.

The new coins differed radically from earlier pieces in omitting the moneyers' names; that of the mint alone sufficed, except on early coins of Bury, which bear the name of Robert de Hadleigh (12).

The excellent quality of Edward's coinage gave rise to a great deal of imitation, especially in Flanders (42–45). These copies entered England in considerable numbers. They were tolerated at first, but the order of 1299 commanding their demonetization and recoinage produced the second great wave of Edwardian coinage (27–31). This was itself widely copied; some of the imitations, such as those of John of Luxembourg (46,47), enjoyed a bad name for baseness. Coinage of identical type continued through the reign of Edward II (1307–27) (35–41) into the first years of Edward III (see Chap. 13). Similar pieces were also struck by the Scots kings (see Chap. 28), and the complicated history of the border town of Berwick is reflected in its highly individual coinage (32–34).

46

34

# 13. Edward III, 1327-77

The earliest coins of Edward III (1,2) differ only in detail from those of Edward II. With the growth of his Continental interests, and in particular his determination to assert his claim to the throne of France, Edward soon came to require a coinage of greater complexity. His first gold coins, of 1344, the Florin, of six shillings (or 72 pence), the Leopard and the Helm (3–5), were unsuccessful. The Noble of six shillings and eight pence (1346), with its half and quarter, were brilliantly successful. The type of the king in a ship evoked an immediate response, and was readily understood as an allusion to maritime power as well as a symbol of government (8).

The noble and its associated issues are classified according to their chronological relationship with the Treaty of Brétigny (1360), by which Edward temporarily gave up his title of King of France. 'Pre-Treaty' nobles (8,21) bear the title 'King of England and France, Lord of Ireland.' 'Treaty' issues, of 1360–69, entitle the King, 'King of England, Lord of Ireland and Guienne'. After the repudiation of the treaty, the full style, 'King of England and France, Lord of Ireland and Guienne', is employed.

Coinage was struck for the king mainly at London, in the Tower. Here were minted all groats (24) and half-groats (two pence), except for a few at Calais (31). The mints of York and Durham, and the rarely-used establishment at Reading (15), were sustained solely by the privileges of the Archbishop, Bishop and Abbot. During the fourteenth and fifteenth centuries, a sensible arrangement left the main bulk of pence to be coined by the ecclesiastical mints, which were in any case not permitted at this time to coin higher denominations.

Some very fine pieces were struck by the King's southern French possessions, both in his own name (7) and in that of his eldest son, Edward the Black Prince (27).

8

11

19

27

32

36

# 14. The House of Lancaster, 1377-1461

Richard II (1377–99) continued the coinage precisely as it had been in his grandfather's last years (1–9). The only extensive provincial issues were the numerous pence of York (6,8); these were struck sometimes from dies produced in London, but often from ones locally made. This practice, the legal basis of which is not known, continued in subsequent reigns. A little coinage was struck in Richard's name in France (10).

The coins of Henry IV (1399–1413) (11–17) are rare, partly because few were struck, and partly because a reduction in the weight of gold and silver coins, carried out in 1411, had, by the time of Henry's death, little effect on the amount of coins in circulation. The inadequate supply of small change in this reign led to the brief but widespread acceptance as halfpence of Venetian *soldini* brought in with the trading fleet to Southampton. However, these so-called 'Galley-halfpence' (16) were declared to be not legal tender.

Henry V (1413–22) (18–22) altered the coinage in detail only. His nobles (18) are distinguished by the omission of the title 'Lord of Guienne', and the classification of lower denominations is based on comparison with them. By the Treaty of Troyes (1420), Henry renounced the title of King of France, being recognised as heir to the French throne in right of his wife. Although the English coins take no account of this event, his latest issues in his extensive lands in northern France style him 'King of England, Heir of France' (22).

An abundant coinage, both in gold and silver (23–28), was struck for Henry VI (1422–61) in the first few years of his reign. Later issues reflect his growing financial difficulties, and are much less common. They are distinguished and defined by the presence of characteristic heraldic symbols in the design or between certain words. Of particular interest are the fine Salutes of his French coinage; the Virgin Mary and the Archangel Gabriel are seen as symbols of France and England, united under Henry's rule (36). Henry was dethroned in 1461, but restored briefly in 1470–71. The rare coins struck during this period (37) conform to the reduced standard of weight introduced by Edward IV in 1465.

8

16

1

4

18

23

# 15. The House of York, 1461-85

For a short time at the start of his reign, Edward IV (1461–83) struck a small number of coins to the standard introduced by Henry V (7). Most of his coinage, however, was struck to a lighter standard. In spite of these weight reductions, the gold noble was now valued at eight shillings and four pence, and a change in standard was accompanied by a review of denominations. The type of the King in a ship was maintained on a slightly larger coin of ten shillings, the Ryal or Rose Noble, distinguished by a rose on the ship's side (1,2). Though the denomination proved short-lived in England, it acquired a special position in Continental trade with the Baltic; many copies were produced, especially in Flanders (6), in the succeeding century. The useful denomination of six shillings and eight pence was revived for a new coin, the Angel (4,5), so called from its representation of St Michael slaying a dragon. The angel achieved immediate popularity, and was the gold coin in general use for the next sixty years or more (see Chap. 16).

Several new mints were created or revived to carry out the recoinage of earlier gold and silver in 1465 (9–12). They lasted only a few years, though the ecclesiastical mints of York and Durham were as active as ever in the coinage of pence (17,18), and the mint of the Archbishop of Canterbury was reactivated (14). An unusual supplement to the currency in this reign were the Double Patards of Burgundy (21), which were permitted to circulate in England.

The very rare coins attributed to Edward V (1483) (22–24) and the somewhat more extensive coinage of Richard III (1483–85) (25–30) present no unusual features. Most coins now bore a heraldic device at the commencement of their inscriptions. These marks, known as 'privy marks', were developed from those in use under Henry VI, and defined groups of coins struck in the same period. They were employed to facilitate the identification of coins at the Trial of the Pyx, and this may have been their purpose from the start.

30

21

1

7

14

28

35

36

# 16. The Early Tudors, 1485-1547

The coinage of Henry VII (1485–1509) was the first to make a significant break with medieval traditions. The normal gold coin throughout the reign was the angel (2–4), but a notable innovation, struck first in 1489 and thereafter never long abandoned, was the Sovereign of twenty shillings (1). The splendid effigy of the King enthroned, not seen on an English coin since Henry III (Chap. 11, no.22), was also, rather oddly, used for the tiny penny (22), which introduced the royal arms as the standard reverse type of the silver coinage. The series of groats (5–13) illustrates the steady development of Henry's effigy from the conventional face established under Edward I towards the Renaissance-style portrait of his last years. The portrait groats of his last issue were accompanied by a yet larger silver coin, the Testoon of twelve pence (14), the ancestor of our modern shilling, but this, like Edward I's groat (Chap. 12), was ahead of its time, and failed to establish itself.

In his toleration, and indeed extension, of ecclesiastical coinage, however, Henry retained a conservative policy (16,17,20–22).

For the first seventeen years of his reign, Henry VIII (1509–47) merely continued his father's policy (24–27), not even substituting his own portrait for that of Henry VII on the groats and half-groats (26). In 1526 a reform brought the gold currency into line with that of France. As in the time of Edward III, a false start was made (31), but the Crown of the Double Rose (32–36) soon replaced the angel as the normal gold coin in circulation. Sovereigns continued to be struck in small numbers (29), but the short-lived George Noble (28,30) was soon discontinued. On the silver coins, the portrait of Henry VIII now appeared (37–42), and the ecclesiastical mints had a final burst of activity before closing for ever (39–42). The groat struck by Cardinal Wolsey when Archbishop of York (39) has a special interest; he had no right to coin anything larger than a half-groat, and the charges against him duly included this offence.

39

42

6

12

15

# 17. Debasement and Recovery

The last years of Henry VIII were marked by an unprecedented debasement of the coinage. The gold coinage fell in weight and in fineness by nearly 20 per cent (1–4). The silver suffered even worse, the alloy declining rapidly from 75 per cent fine, to 50 and finally 33 per cent. The debased silver coins were distinguished sharply from earlier issues by the formidable facing portrait of the king; this took two principal forms, a fully frontal design on the twelve-penny testoons (6) and a slightly oblique representation on the groats (5,7,8,11). In order to produce enough of the new coinage, the former ecclesiastical mints of Canterbury and York (8,9) were revived as royal establishments and new mints were created at Southwark and Bristol (7,11).

Down to 1550 the coinage of Edward VI (1547–53) was base and confused. Some issues bore the name of Henry VIII (20), others that of Edward himself. Towards the end of 1550, a new and much improved coinage heralded the end of debasement. The silver coins returned to the sterling alloy (92·5 per cent) and, with their 'gothic' lettering and new types, made a deliberate break with the immediate past. The crowns and half-crowns (24,25), with the monarch on horseback, introduced a new dimension to the silver coinage, while the elegant shillings, sixpences and threepences (26–28) were the first English coins to state their value.

Mary's reign (1553–58) was divided into two parts by her marriage to Philip II of Spain. Before her marriage she was shown with flowing hair (30–32). Later groats and half-groats continued Philip and Mary's name with the portrait of Mary alone (33,36), but the shillings and sixpences (34,35) depicted the monarchs facing each other, on the model of the Spanish gold coins of Ferdinand and Isabella, the queen's grandparents. An issue of base pence (37) was the last silver coinage not of sterling standard issued for England down to 1920.

The coming of Renaissance influence to England brought with it the first medals. The two earliest official issues appear to be products of the Royal Mint. That of Henry VIII (12), struck in 1545, is a powerful and ingenious work, but the Coronation medal of Edward VI (13) is poor in concept and slovenly in execution. They had no successors. The best work for English patrons was done by foreign artists. Henry VIII, by Hans Schwarz (14) and Mary, by Jacopo da Trezzo (15), are fine and characteristic achievements.

18

24

30

34

# 18. Elizabeth I, 1558-1603, and James I, 1603-25

The base money of Henry VIII and Edward VI was swept away early in Elizabeth I's reign. Shillings of Edward VI were countermarked with a portcullis (5) or a greyhound (6) according to their fineness, and in 1561 demonetized. A very large issue of shillings (1) and groats (2) between 1558 and 1561, and of sixpences (15) thereafter, set the currency on a sound footing. Following the practice established in 1526, Elizabeth's gold coins were struck at two standards. The sovereign, ryal and angel (7–11) were made of 23 carat 3½ grain gold; the pound, half-pound, crown and half-crown (12–14) of 22 carat gold.

Elizabeth's silver coins introduced an interesting method of distinguishing the denominations. Instead of the numerals used by Edward VI and sometimes by Mary (and revived by James I), alternate denominations between the tiny three-farthings and the shilling were marked on the obverse with a rose and on the reverse with the date.

In the 1560s and 1570s experiments in the making of coins by machinery were undertaken (24,25). However, hand-work was found to be more rapid and accurate, and was not superseded for another century. A project to replace the little silver pence and half-pence by copper pieces resulted in some patterns being struck (26), and another abortive scheme at the end of the reign was the striking of special coins for the trade with the Indies (27). At the same time began the regular coinage of silver crowns and half-crowns (20,21), though gold crowns were not discontinued until the reign of Charles II.

The few medals of this reign naturally concentrate around the Armada expedition of 1588. They are cast pieces in the miniaturist tradition, quite unrelated to the coinage (22,23).

The reign of James I (1603–25) saw the last systematic coinage of 23 carat 3½ grain gold coinage (29,30,44,45). There were a few novelties, such as the Thistle Crown (32) of four shillings, but the main interest lies in the inscriptions. These depart from the scriptural 'I have made God my helper', which with a few similar legends had lasted from Edward III to Elizabeth, and introduce allusions to the union of the English and Scottish crowns. James's last coinage includes the ungainly Laurel (46), with its representation of the King in the guise of a Roman emperor. From James's reign date the first copper farthings (48), coined not by the Royal Mint but by private contractors.

A few medals were made abroad, to celebrate the discovery of the Gunpowder Plot (28), but the most characteristic pieces of the reign are the silver plaques made by Simon Passe (43), honouring the Royal family.

31

43

46

# 19. Charles I, 1625-49

The troubles of Charles I's reign produced an unusually varied and interesting coinage. Issues of all denominations and of normal types continued in London down to his death; in this respect, the Civil Wars brought no change (33,34).

The regular gold coinage ran from the Unite of twenty shillings to the crown of five shillings (1–4). The gold half-crown had been discontinued in 1618, and its silver equivalent was now a normal part of the currency (6,7). Silver crowns (5) remained exceptional until the reign of Charles II. Abundant issues of half-crowns and shillings (8) were made during the latter part of the reign, especially in the early years of the Civil War. The output of sixpences (9) was much less, and finds show that this denomination was mostly supplied by the massive issues of Elizabeth. The finer standard of gold was now represented only by the angel (10,14), which was extremely rare, and generally survives pierced for use as a 'touch piece' – the coin presented by the King to those touched by him at healing ceremonies. They were naturally discontinued when the King lost control of London at the outbreak of the wars in 1642.

Experiments in the manufacture of coins by machinery were resumed under Charles. Nicholas Briot, who had unsuccessfully attempted to have his machines accepted in France, came to England and struck an extensive series of patterns (13–18). Though his efforts had little effect on the regular coinage, his machines were shipped to York and served the King until 1644 (Chap. 20).

No less significant was the mint at Aberystwyth, opened by Thomas Bushell in 1638. Down to mid-1637, the silver mined by Bushell in Wales had been transported to London, and coins struck from it were marked with the emblematic plume (23,24). The new mint, which seems to have used machinery, struck a very comprehensive series of denominations in silver from half-crown to halfpenny (25–32). At the start of the Civil Wars it was transferred first to Shrewsbury and then to Oxford (Chap. 20).

Copper farthings continued to be produced by contractors. The machines which made them in effect printed them on strips of metal, from which the coins were punched (19,20). The farthings were much faked, and in an effort to render this more difficult, later issues were made with brass inserts in the copper flan (21).

Medals underwent a considerable development in this reign. National occasions were now more often celebrated (11,37), and many fine pieces commemorate public men (12,22,35,36).

# 20. The Civil Wars and the Commonwealth, 1642–60

The nature of the coinage after 1642 was conditioned by Parliament's possession of the Tower Mint (Chap. 19, nos.33,34). Charles I's principal mint was the Aberystwyth establishment, moved in 1642 to Shrewsbury (3,7) and thence to Oxford (1,2,4). Its issues were sporadic, depending on fortuitous supplies of bullion and plate, and included some unusually large denominations – the Triple Unite (1) in gold and the pound and half-pound (2) in silver. Types were propagandist in character, suggesting the King's desire for peace but resolution in war, and advertising his declaration that he would stand by 'The Protestant Religion, the Laws of England and the Liberty of Parliament'. Other needs were supplied by a mint at York (10, see Chap. 19) and by a succession of West Country establishments (5–9).

A number of towns and castles under siege are known to have struck coins. Those of Chester (16) are normal in type and fabric, those of Newark (19–22) are diamond-shaped, while those of Carlisle (18) and Pontefract (24–26) vary. Issues continued down to and even after the execution of Charles I in 1649 (23–26).

Medals of this period were mostly badges, with portraits of the leading figures of each party (11–15), but later a few historical allusions appear, such as to the victory of Cromwell at Dunbar (28) and the Scottish coronation of Charles II in 1651 (27). The medal commemorating Charles I's execution (35) was, of course, struck long after the event.

The coinage of the Commonwealth (1649–60) was remarkable for its legends being entirely in English. Its unattractive type of two shields was scoffed at for resembling a pair of breeches, 'a fit stamp for the coin of the Rump' (29–31); it was rapidly withdrawn after the Restoration. Signs of improvement were, however, apparent in the patterns – machine-made gold and silver pieces in the name of Cromwell (32,33), and a considerable series of copper farthings (34).

1

47

3

10

14

# 21. The Restoration, 1660-88

With the return to Britain of Charles II (1660–85), celebrated by a series of fine medals made in Holland as well as England (1,2), coinage in the old manner was not long continued (3–5). There was competition as to who should cut the dies for the proposed machine-made coinage. Thomas Simon, who had produced the portrait dies of Cromwell (Chap. 20, nos.32,33), created the celebrated 'Petition Crown' (8), a remarkable *tour-de-force,* but it was the less flamboyantly Baroque style of John Roettier which eventually found favour.

The money system of 1663, which lasted until 1817 (Chap 23), was based on the Guinea of twenty shillings. Gold coins were of five (9), two, and one guinea, as well as a half-guinea. The silver crown now entirely superseded its gold counterpart. Gold and silver coins were closely similar in type, and fraudulent gilding of the silver was prevented by minor, though distinct, differences on obverse and reverse (9,10). The new issues were by no means a recoinage; the old hammered silver coins remained current until 1696, the gold until 1733. The guineas, whose value (like that of earlier gold coins) rose and fell with the price of gold, soon became an integral part of the currency. The silver, which found itself alongside earlier issues worn and clipped far below the original standard, but of the same face value, disappeared into hoards or was melted down.

The only reform which had immediate and lasting effect was the suppression in 1672 of the mass of local tradesmen's tokens (26–28) and their replacement by fine copper halfpence and farthings (13,14), the first English coins to bear the figure of Britannia.

From the beginning of the reign come some excellent portrait medals (6,7) by Abraham Simon. Later on, the finest examples were by John Roettier; his best-known work is of the Duchess of Richmond, posing as Britannia (11,12).

The coinage of James II (1685–88) continued with little change (16–23). Of some importance are the silver coins from groat to penny (18–21); the extensive issue of these denominations had been revived in 1670, and they are the ancestors of our Maundy Money. Another legacy from the end of the previous reign were halfpence and farthings struck in tin (22,23). They were a short-lived attempt to utilize native English tin for coinage, and contained a copper plug to prevent confusion with the silver.

The principal medallist of the reign was George Bower. His work, though historically interesting, verges on the grotesque (15,24,25).

22

15

27

11

5

21

25

34

43

# 22. The Glorious Revolution, 1688-1727

The joint reign of William III and Mary (1688–94) and the reigns of William III (1694–1702) and Anne (1702–14) were times of war, principally against France. An early medal (1) recalls William's embarkation for England, while others celebrate incidents in the wars in Ireland (2,3) and at sea (4). Down to 1694 the king and queen are represented with superimposed portraits (5–12), the only important change being the final abandonment of tin for copper in the halfpence and farthings (10–12).

William's sole reign is notable for the recall and recoinage of the old hammered silver. The clipping of this, which in 1652 was estimated to have reduced its weight by some 25 per cent, had by 1694 diminished it by almost 50 per cent. Between November 1694 and June 1695 guineas (13) rose in value to thirty shillings, reflecting the public desire for a return to a bullion relationship between gold and the silver coin in actual circulation. This was an interesting phenomena at a time when events had lowered confidence in the stability and credit of William's régime and the unclippable milled silver money had disappeared into hoards. The hammered silver coins were demonetized and recoined between 1695 and 1697, additional mints being opened at Bristol, Chester, Exeter, Norwich and York (18–22) to expedite this. Guineas soon fell below twenty-two shillings in value, and were finally stabilized at twenty-one shillings in 1717.

Little change took place under Anne. The Act of Union in 1707 between England and Scotland was reflected in medals (25) and in the cessation of a separate Scottish coinage (Chap. 28). A silver coinage of English type at Edinburgh (29) swept away the surviving Scots coin. From the time of James I it had been the practice to denote on the coinage the origin of exceptional sources of metal. The legend 'Vigo' (24,27,30) records the bullion captured in Vigo Bay in 1702. The French Wars and the Duke of Marlborough, the great British commander, were commemorated on medals (35,36), and the Peace of Utrecht, which terminated the war, was also celebrated on pattern farthings of 1713 (32–34). It is unlikely that the famous farthings were ever made current.

George I (1714–27) was fortunate in sharing with Anne the services of the medallist John Croker (37), one of the finest to work in England. The Jacobite revolt of 1715 (38) left no mark on the coinage, which was otherwise chiefly remarkable for the drying up of the supply of silver to the mint, except for such adventitious sources as the South Sea Company (43) and the Welsh Copper Company (44), and silver of mixed Welsh and West Country origin (45). In an attempt to supply the lack of silver coin, tiny quarter-guineas (42) were struck.

# 23. George II, 1727-60 and George III, 1760-1820

Throughout the reign of George II and most of his successor's, the currency consisted largely of gold and copper. The scanty silver issues were mostly made from occasional sources, like the bullion brought back by Anson after his voyage round the world (7), and the small amounts of English and Welsh metal (10,11). Virtually no silver coins were issued between 1758 and 1816 (35–37). The medals of the reign are interesting and important. Some celebrate events of national interest (2,16,17), others honour statesmen and soldiers (14,18). An interesting group, whose abundance indicates the popularity of the subject, refers to successes against the Spaniards in the West Indies, and in particular to the exploits of Admiral Vernon (12,13).

By the start of George III's reign (1760–1820), the currency had fallen into a very unsatisfactory condition. The last of the old hammered gold, including pieces going back to the time of Henry VIII, was recoined in 1733. By 1773 so light had the older guineas become that a further recoinage, based on weight, left few in circulation earlier than about 1730. Gold was not however scarce, and there were abundant issues of guineas and half-guineas (23,24) and after 1800 of third-guineas also (31). Negligible amounts of silver were struck (25); attempts to supplement the shortage by countermarked (28) or overstruck (29) Spanish dollars merely stimulated forgery on a vast scale. The copper coinage was also extensively imitated and, as in the seventeenth century, it was accompanied by numerous tokens (42,43) many of them little better than forgeries.

Beginning in 1797, spasmodic issues of well-struck coppers (26,27,30), including the first copper pence, gradually put the low value currency on to a proper footing. Gold and silver were at last brought into a proper relationship by the reforms of 1816–17, which replaced the guinea by the sovereign (33,34), and established a gold standard, against which the silver coinage (35–37) had a token and not a bullion value.

As in the previous reign, the medals commemorate statesmen and soldiers (19–22, 38–41), but few have much artistic merit.

7

12

24

27

28

34

42

21

38

# 24. The Last Hanoverians, 1820-37

In the last years of George III and at the beginning of the reign of George IV (1820-30), the leading engraver was Benedetto Pistrucci, creator of the St George and Dragon motif (Chap. 23, nos.33,35), and of the grandiose though unfulfilled Waterloo medal (1). It is not surprising that Pistrucci's uncompromisingly realistic, and unattractive, portrait (2-10) became intolerable to the King, who was fortunate that so talented an artist as William Wyon was prepared to work in a blander style (11-15). An unusual feature of the currency was the double-sovereign (2); together with its numerous brass copies, this became a favourite ornament on watch-chains, and gave rise to a proverb in early Victorian times: 'from a two-pound piece to a farthing'.

Men of letters and engineers now joined the ranks of those commemorated by medals (16-18), and the railway, the new wonder of the age (19), was recorded in much topographic detail.

The coinage of William IV (1830-37) offers no remarkable feature other than the revival of the groat. This was given the type of Britannia (25) and a grained edge (c. Chap. 25, no.12); contrast the threepence, which bore the mark of value within a wreath (30). The Maundy coins retained their traditional type of the numeral (29-32). The mantled arms of the half-crown (23) did not survive the reign, whilst the Britannia reverse (26) on the copper coinage continued unaltered until 1860.

The important social and political events of William's reign were duly celebrated by popular medals. Many commemorate the Reform of Parliament in 1832 (33), but the abolition of slavery (35), and the new railways (34), are not overlooked.

I

I

4

12

20

22

# 25. Victoria, The Early Years 1837-1860

Victoria (1837–1901), 'England's Opening Rose' (1), was greeted as a welcome change (2,3) from the unlikeable men of the Hanoverian line. The times were ripe for her to be represented in a romantic (4,14), even medieval way (22–24). Despite this, however, her coinage continued for much of the reign in a neo-classical manner (5–13, 15–17), under the influence of the elder Wyon (see Chap. 24); although it was he who produced the fully-developed Gothic Revival style (22–24) used for the florin, intended as a tentative step towards decimalization. Leonard Wyon, his successor, favoured the romantic style for the new bronze coinage of 1860 (25–27).

Victoria's accession came suddenly; an interesting pair of medals (2,3) illustrate the haste and ingenuity with which the unskilful engraver of a popular piece altered his dies to change the Princess, 'England's Hope', into 'England's Queen'. Typical of the official medals (14) is a heavy allegorical style. The more popular pieces, particularly of the early part of the reign, are realistic and informative. Examples show the new Houses of Parliament, rebuilt in 1842 after a destructive fire (18), and the steamship *Great Britain* (20), giving full details of size, capacity and power. Railway architecture continued for a while to attract the medallist (19,29), but it was by now becoming commonplace. Perhaps the most widely celebrated marvel was the 1851 Great Exhibition, and especially its Crystal Palace. The building, both at its Hyde Park and Sydenham sites, and the genius of Sir Joseph Paxton, its designer, received generous tribute (30,31). The more spiritual aspirations of the age were not forgotten. The work of the London Missionary Society in bringing the light of the Gospel to the heathen is represented absurdly, but with sincerity (28). The Madonna-like vision of Florence Nightingale (32) tells us much about Victorian romanticism and its attitude to women, if little about her determined character.

25

28

32

30

# 26. Victoria: The Later Years

The later years of Victoria saw the decline of the romantic 'medieval' style. Coin portraiture now exhibited ornate realism, seen too in much of the medallic art (15). A few fine portraits still reflected direct classical influence (13,14), but they were essentially old-fashioned, as can be clearly seen when they were combined with reverses of advanced style (14). A motif borrowed from the early· part of the reign (see Chap. 25, no.31) is the portrait shown as though within a frame. The influence of photography is evident in the vignette portraits of the Prince of Wales and Alexandra of Denmark on the occasion of their wedding (12).

Architectural types still occur; a fine example celebrates the opening of Tower Bridge in 1894 (19). Note however the 'impressionist' background, unlike the needle-sharp detail of the previous generation. This blurring of detail even invades the coin-portraits after 1893, and is characteristic of much medallic art from the later 1880s until after the First World War. *Art nouveau* left surprisingly few direct traces on the English medal. The International Fisheries Exhibition reverse (14) is a rare example, though we see it more discreetly on the reverse of the elegant Diamond Jubilee medal (20).

The coinage falls into two groups. The Jubilee issues of 1887–92 combine a realistic effigy with a mass of ornate detail (1–11). The resemblance to the later portraiture of Elizabeth I was probably intentional, but it was little admired. The series is remarkable mainly for the double-florin (6), a new denomination that found no favour and was not repeated. Victoria's last coinage (16–18, 21–30) softened and ennobled the features of the old queen.

14

19

# 27. The Twentieth Century, 1901 to decimalisation

The potential stylistic defects of Victoria's last coinage (Chap. 26) are plainly apparent on the undistinguished issues of Edward VII (1901-10). The florin (4) alone offers a novelty, Britannia standing on a ship. Medals also follow the trend of the preceding reign (11,12), an amalgam of impressionism and *art nouveau*.

The coinage of George V (1910–36) falls into two groups. The first is a direct continuation of that of Edward VII (13–22). Gold ceased to be struck regularly in England in 1917; from 1871, sovereigns were also coined in Australia (15–17) and other overseas mints, but these too came to an end soon after the Great War. In 1920 the sterling silver standard was abandoned for the first time since the reign of Mary Tudor (see Chap. 17). The types at first remained unaltered, though the fine silver coin was rapidly withdrawn. In 1927 new types in a more robust style were created (23–28); a special crown piece (29) in a curiously wooden style was produced in honour of the Silver Jubilee of 1935. The bronze coinage remained virtually unchanged throughout the reign. Interesting varieties are those marked with letters denoting that they were struck under contract in the Midlands (31,32). Similar production of some of the copper and bronze coinage under contract was carried out under George III and Victoria. The impressionist style is dominant in the medals of this reign (36–38).

The coinage of Edward VIII (1936) was never made current; had it been, it would have introduced the twelve-sided brass threepence, which was first issued in 1937 (52). Many medals were struck in anticipation of his Coronation (39), and a few to commemorate his Abdication (40).

Down to 1946 the coinage of George VI (1936–52) retained an alloy of 50 per cent silver (42,44,46–49,51), but from 1947, silver was abandoned, except for Maundy Money (69–72), and was replaced by cupro-nickel (43,45,50). In 1937 began the practice of striking two types of shilling (47,48,62,63), one with specific reference to Scotland. A distinctive post-war development has been the striking of commemorative crowns (43,56–58). Novel types were introduced in the halfpenny and farthing (54,55), Drake's ship 'The Golden Hind', and the tiny wren.

Down to 1970 the coinage of the present reign (56–72) offered no new features, except for the portcullis type of the brass threepence (65). The complete break with tradition, both in types and denominations, that has come with the decimal series makes 1970 a natural end to a historical exhibition.

36

52

54

55

56

58

69

70

71

72

# 28. Scotland and Ireland

The earliest Scots pence were minted under David I (1124–53), but those prior to the reign of William I, the Lion (1165–1214) (1) are very rare. A large proportion was struck at Border mints such as Berwick and Roxburgh, and economically it constitutes a mere extension of the coinage of the mints of northern England. Throughout the later thirteenth and fourteenth centuries, Scots coinage closely follows the types and standards of contemporary England (2–7).

By the fifteenth century Scotland had given up the struggle to keep her coinage at parity with that of England. Silver coins, sometimes of base metal, retain English types with only slight modifications (9,11,12), but the gold developed a native typology with St Andrew, and the Lion (8) and Unicorn (10).

James V (1513–42) tried in the middle years of his reign to assimilate his gold and silver standards to those of Henry VIII (15). His final coinage, however, (14,16) gave up the attempt. The varied coinage of Mary (1542–67) illustrates the successive constitutional changes in her reign (17–21), while that of James VI (1567–1625) shows his efforts to adjust the Scots coinage to the English standard (22–25). The Scots pound was by this time worth only one twelfth of that of England.

Between 1603 and 1706 special issues continued to be made for Scotland (26). Following the Act of Union (1707), the Edinburgh mint restruck the old money into the standard type (Chap. 22, no.29) and then closed.

Irish coinage begins with the issues of Sihtric (c. 995–1020), the Norse King of Dublin (27). These were extensively copied in later years (28), but it was not until the later twelfth century that regular issues recommenced. These began in the name of John, as Lord of Ireland (1172–99), and then as

2

6

10

14

19

27

30

34

King (1199–1216) (Chap. 11, no.21). Similar pence with the bust in a triangle were struck by his successors (Chap. 11, no.35). Thereafter, no special coins were struck for Ireland until the later fifteenth century, when fairly extensive issues of very poorly produced pieces were made (31–33).

The sixteenth century saw the introduction of the harp to the coinage as a symbol of Ireland. It was also a period in which the country first shared in the English debasement (see Chap. 17), and then retained the base coin after the English recovery (34–37). Under James I (1603–25) there was an improvement; shillings of good silver were struck (38), though their weight was so low that in England they passed only for ninepence.

During the Civil Wars, a good deal of roughly-produced silver coin appeared (39,40), much of it anonymous and inscribed only with weight and value. Thereafter only copper coins were struck for Ireland (41–47). During the short lived occupation of parts of Ireland by James II (1685–90), a base metal coinage of high nominal value was issued (42). This so-called 'Gun-money' became worthless with the King's flight. Irish coinage came to an end in 1823, and was not resumed until 1928.

42

45

# Select Bibliography

**Brooke, G. C.** *English Coins from the Seventh Century to the Present Day.* London, 3rd. ed., 1952.

**Carson, R. A. G.** *Coins: ancient, medieval, modern.* London, 1962.

**Grueber, H. A.** *Handbook of the Coins of Great Britain and Ireland.* 2nd. ed., London, 1972.

**Hawkins, E.** ed. **Franks, A. W.** and **Grueber, H. A.** *Medallic Illustrations of the History of Great Britain and Ireland to the death of George III.* London, 1885; reprinted London, 1969.

**Mack, R. P.** *The Coinage of Ancient Britain.* 2nd. ed., London, 1964.

**Mattingly, H.** *Roman Coins.* 2nd. ed., London, 1960.

# List of Coins Illustrated

## 1 Celtic Britain

1 Philip II of Macedon (351–336 BC); gold
  stater.
2 Gallo-Belgic gold stater, Class A, c.70 BC.
7 British gold stater, Class A, c.55 BC.
25 Cunobelinus, gold stater, c.AD 20.
33 Silver coin of the Iceni, first century AD.
35 'Speculum' coin, South-east England, first
  century BC.

## 2 Roman Britain

2 Claudius I (AD 41–54); gold aureus.
10 Hadrian (117–138); brass sestertius.
12 Septimius Severus (193–211); silver denarius.
22 Tetricus I (271–274); barbarous copy of a
  base silver coin.
24 Claudius II, posthumous base silver coin,
  c.270–271.
26,27 Base silver coins (330–335),
  commemorating the foundation of
  Constantinople.
30 Constans (337–350); base silver coin.

## 3 Rebels in Britain

3 Carausius (286–293); base silver coin.
11 Carausius; base medallion.
12 Carausius; silver 'denarius'.
14 Carausius; base silver coin.
36 Allectus (293–296); gold aureus.
43 Allectus; base silver coin.

## 4 The London Mint in Roman Times

1 Diocletian (284–305); base silver follis.
15 Maximian (307–310); base silver follis.
22 Constantine I (306–337); base silver follis.
37 Constantine I; base silver follis.
55 Constantine I; base silver centenionalis.
63 Helena; base silver centenionalis, c.325.
64 Fausta; base silver centenionalis, c.325.
65 Magnus Maximus (383–388); gold solidus.

## 5 The First Coins of the English

5 Merovingian gold tremissis in the name of
  Justin II (565–578).
12 Base gold Anglo-Saxon tremissis, moneyer
  Pada, c. late seventh century.
16 Anglo-Saxon silver penny (sceatta), early
  eighth century.
24 Charlemagne (768–814); gold solidus.
28 Offa (757–796); silver penny.
29 Cynethryth, wife of Offa; silver penny.
75 Copy of a gold Arab dinar of 774, with the
  name of Offa,

## 6 Mercia and Kent

1 Coenwulf (796–821); silver penny.
6 Ludica (825–827); silver penny.
9 Burgred (852–874); silver penny.
12 Cuthred (798–807); silver penny.
17 Wulfred (806–832); silver penny.
20 Plegmund (890–914); silver penny.

## 7 East Anglia, Northumbria and the Vikings

2 Aethelberht (c.794); silver penny.
8 Guthrum (Aethelstan II 880–890); silver
  penny.
10 Viking silver penny in the name of
  St Edmund (c.880–910).
15 King Eadberht and Archbishop Ecgberht
  (737–758); silver penny (styca).
20 Eanred (808–841); base silver penny (styca).
27 Archbishop Wigmund (837–854); gold
  solidus.
38 Anlaf (941–944); silver penny.

## 8 Wessex

2 Ecgbeorht (802–839); silver penny.
6 Aelfred (871–899); 'offering penny'.
9 Aelfred; silver penny, London mint.
23 Eadwerd the Elder (899–925); silver penny.
28 Silver penny in the name of Howel Dda
  (c.904–949), Chester mint.

## 9 Kings of All England

1 Edgar (959–975); silver penny, Derby mint.
14 Ethelred II (979–1016); silver penny, Exeter
  mint.
18 Cnut (1016–35); silver penny, Bath mint.
21 Harold I (1035–40); silver penny, Thetford
  mint.
22 Harthacnut (1040–42); silver penny, Oxford
  mint.
31 Edward the Confessor (1042–66); silver
  penny, Canterbury mint.
38 Harold II (1066); silver penny, Chichester
  mint.

**10 The Normans**

14 William I, the Conqueror (1066–87); silver penny, Hereford mint.
16 William II (1087–1100); silver penny, London mint.
33 Henry I (1100–35); silver penny, London mint.
35 Stephen (1135–54); silver penny, Thetford mint.
44 Stephen and Queen Matilda; silver penny, York mint.
45 Empress Matilda; silver penny, c.1141, Oxford mint.
46 Eustace FitzJohn; silver penny, York mint.

**11 The early Plantagenets**

1 Henry II (1154–89); silver penny ('Tealby' type), Newcastle mint.
5 Silver penny (short cross type), Northampton mint.
20 Richard I (1189–99); silver denier of Aquitaine.
21 John (1199–1216); Irish silver penny, Dublin mint.
22 Henry III (1216–72); gold penny, London mint.
29 Henry III; silver penny (long cross type), Newcastle mint.
35 Henry III; Irish penny, Dublin mint.
*(All coins hereafter are London mint unless otherwise stated.)*

**12 Edward I and Edward II**

3,12 Edward I (1272–1307); silver pennies, London and Bury St Edmunds mints.
19 Edward I; silver groat.
23 Edward I; silver halfpenny.
24 Edward I; silver farthing.
34 Edward I; silver penny, Berwick mint.
35 Edward II (1307–27); silver penny, Durham mint.
42 Gui de Dampierre, Count of Flanders (1280–1305); silver sterling.
46 John the Blind, Count of Luxembourg (1309–46); silver sterling.

**13 Edward III, 1327–77**

3 Gold Florin.
7 Gold Guiennois (of Aquitaine), 1361–62.
8 Gold Noble.
24 Silver groat.
27 Edward the Black Prince; demi gros of Aquitaine, Poitiers mint.

**14 The House of Lancaster**

8 Richard II (1377–99); silver penny, York mint.
11 Henry IV (1399–1413); gold Noble.
16 Silver Venetian soldino ('Galley-halfpenny') of Doge Michele Steno (1400–13).
19 Henry V (1413–22); silver groat.
27 Henry VI (1422–61); silver groat, Calais mint.
36 Henry VI; gold Salute, St Lô mint.

**15 The House of York**

1 Edward IV (1461–83); gold Ryal (Rose Noble).
4 Gold Angel.
18 Silver penny, York mint.
21 Silver double patard of Flanders. Charles the Bold (1468–77).
23 Edward V (1483); silver groat.
30 Richard III (1483–85); silver penny, Durham mint.

**16 The Early Tudors**

1 Henry VII (1485–1509); gold sovereign.
7 Silver groat.
14 Silver Testoon (shilling).
28 Henry VIII (1509–47); gold George Noble.
35 Gold Crown of the Double Rose.
39 Silver groat, York mint.
42 Silver half groat, Canterbury mint.

**17 Debasement and Recovery**

6 Silver Testoon.
12 Gold medal of Henry VIII as Head of the English church (1545).
15 Queen Mary (1555); gold medal.
18 Edward VI (1547–53); gold half sovereign.
24 Silver crown.
30 Mary (1553–58); gold Ryal.
34 Philip and Mary; silver shilling, 1554.

**18 Elizabeth I and James I**

7 Elizabeth I (1558–1603); gold sovereign.
22 Elizabeth I; gold Armada medal (1588).
25 Milled silver sixpence, 1566.
26 Pattern for a penny, 1601.
31 James I (1603–25); sovereign (Unite).
43 Silver medal of James I and his family.
46 Gold Laurel.

**19 Charles I, 1625–49**

2 Gold Unite.

10 Gold Angel, pierced for use as a 'touch piece'.

11 Gold medal. Return to London (1633).

18 Silver crown, by Briot.

19 A strip of copper farthings.

25 Silver half crown, Aberystwyth mint.

37 Gold medal. Declaration of Parliament (1642).

**20 The Civil War and the Commonwealth**

1 Charles I; gold Triple Unite (three pounds), Oxford mint, 1643.

3 Silver Pound, Shrewsbury mint, 1642.

10 Silver half crown, York mint (1642–44).

14 Silver medal of Sir Thomas Fairfax (1645).

19 Silver half crown, Newark mint, 1646.

26 Charles II; silver shilling, Pontefract mint, 1648.

28 Silver medal of Oliver Cromwell. Battle of Dunbar, 1650.

30 Silver half crown of the Commonwealth, 1651.

**21 The Restoration**

1 Charles II (1660–85); silver medal of embarkation at Scheveningen (1660).

8 Silver crown (the 'Petition Crown'), 1663.

11 Pewter medal. Duchess of Richmond as Britannia (1667).

13 Copper halfpenny, 1672.

15 Silver medal. Defeat of the Duke of Monmouth, 1685.

22 James II (1685–88); tin halfpenny, 1685.

27 Copper token halfpenny of Richard Clarke at The Swan in The Minories, London, 1668.

**22 The Glorious Revolution**

5 William and Mary (1688–94); gold five guinea piece, 1692.

21 William III (1694–1702); silver shilling, Norwich mint, 1697.

25 Queen Anne (1702–14); silver medal, Act of Union, 1707.

34 Copper pattern farthing, 1713.

43 George I (1714–27); silver shilling, 1723.

**23 George II and George III**

7 George II (1727–60); silver 'Lima' crown, 1746.

12 Bronze medal of Admiral Vernon. Capture of Portobello, 1739.

21 Silver medal of William Wilberforce, 1807.

24 George III (1760–1820); gold 'Spade' guinea, 1787.

27 Copper 'cartwheel' twopence, 1797.

28 Silver countermarked Spanish dollar, 1794.

34 Gold half sovereign, 1817.

38 Bronze medal of Lord Nelson. Battle of Trafalgar, 1805.

42 Parys Mines Company, Anglesey; copper token penny, 1787.

**24 The Last Hanoverians**

1 Medal commemorating the Battle of Waterloo (1815).

2 George IV (1820–30); gold double sovereign, 1823.

15 Silver shilling, 1827.

23 William IV (1830–37); silver half crown, 1876.

26 Copper penny, 1874.

34 Liverpool and Manchester Railway, 1834; white metal medal.

**25 Victoria, The Early Years 1837–60**

4 Gold pattern five pound piece. Una and the Lion, 1839.

12 Silver fourpence, 1838.

20 The *Great Britain* launched 1843; bronze medal.

22 Silver 'Gothic' crown, 1847.

25 Bronze 'bun' penny, 1860.

28 London Missionary Society, 1844; white metal medal.

30 The Great Exhibition, 1851; white metal medal.

32 Florence Nightingale (1834); white metal medal.

**26 Victoria, The Later Years 1860–1901**

1 Gold five pound piece, 1887.

12 Wedding of the Prince of Wales, 1863; bronze medal.

14 International Fisheries, 1883; bronze medal.

19 Tower Bridge opened, 1894; bronze medal.

20 Diamond Jubilee, 1897; silver medal.

**The Twentieth Century**

4 Edward VII (1901–10); silver two shillings
(florin), 1903.

11 Silver coronation medal, 1902.

29 George V (1910–36); silver crown of Jubilee,
1935.

36 Silver medal of Lord Kitchener, 1916.

40 Silver medal of Edward VIII; the Abdication
(1936).

52 George VI (1936–52); nickel-brass
threepence, 1937.

54 Bronze halfpenny, 1937.

55 Bronze farthing, 1937.

56 Elizabeth II (1952–); cupro-nickel crown,
1953.

58 Cupro-nickel crown, Churchill, 1965.

69–72 Silver Maundy set, 1972.

**28 Scotland and Ireland**

*Scotland*

2 Alexander III (1249–86); silver penny,
Edinburgh mint.

6 David II (1329–71); silver groat, Edinburgh
mint.

10 James III (1460–88); gold Unicorn,
Edinburgh mint.

14 James V (1530–42); gold 'Bonnet' piece,
1540, Edinburgh mint.

19 Mary; silver Testoon, 1562, Edinburgh
mint.

*Ireland*

27 Sihtric (c.995–1020); Hiberno–Norse silver
penny, Dublin mint.

34 Henry VIII (1509–47); silver 'Harp' groat,
London mint.

40 Charles I (1625–49); silver Ormonde half
crown, Dublin mint.

42 James II (1685–90); 'Gun-money' half
crown, October 1689, Dublin mint.

45 George IV (1820–30); copper penny, 1822,
Soho Mint, Birmingham.